Amebic Dysentery

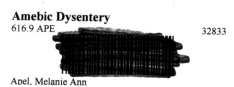

MELANIE ANN APEL

Epidemics

Deadly Diseases
Throughout History

AMEBIC DYSENTERY

The Rosen Publishing Group, Inc.
New York

Published in 2004 by The Rosen Publishing Group, Inc.
29 East 21st Street, New York, NY 10010

Library of Congress Cataloging-in-Publication Data

Apel, Melanie Ann.
Amebic dysentery / by Melanie Ann Apel.— 1st ed.
    p. cm. — (Epidemics)
Summary: Discusses amebic dysentery, examining how one gets it, how to treat it, and its symptoms.
Includes bibliographical references and index.
ISBN 0-8239-4196-5 (lib. bdg.)
1. Amebiasis—Juvenile literature. [1. Dysentery. 2. Diseases.]
I. Title. II. Series.
RC121.A5A64 2004
616.9'353—dc21

                                    2003000823

Manufactured in the United States of America

Cover image: A close-up of *Entamoeba histolytica*

CONTENTS

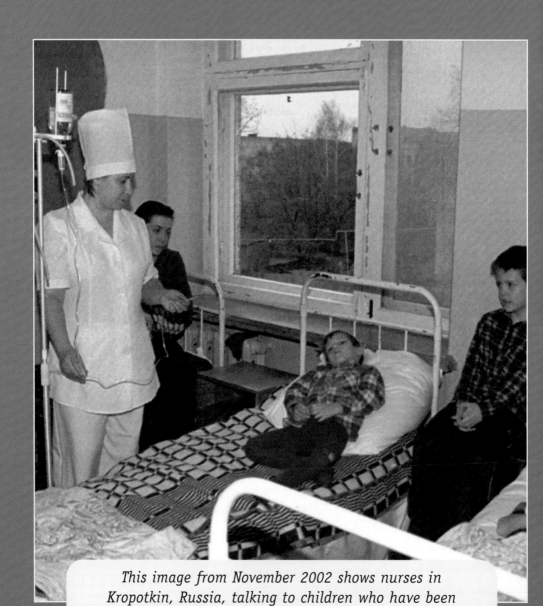

This image from November 2002 shows nurses in Kropotkin, Russia, talking to children who have been hospitalized for amebic dysentery.

INTRODUCTION

*I*t was September 1990. My wife, Mary, and I were on a safari trip to Kenya and Tanzania in Africa. We went during the dry season and it was not particularly hot. My wife and I had been warned ahead of time to take food and drink precautions: We knew not to have ice in our drinks, not to eat salads and other raw fruits and vegetables, and to eat only well-cooked foods. We brought several bottles of Pepto-Bismol from home. We also took care to get the full range of shots, including one for hepatitis, before we left the United States for our safari. We really believed we were well prepared for our adventure.

The tour was in two parts. We went to Kenya first, then on to Tanzania. It happened near the end of the first leg of the trip during the final *days we were in Kenya. It had to be a meal we ate at one of the lodges, very likely the salad we had. The strange thing is Mary and I ate exactly the same foods up to the point I became sick. All but two people in our tour group became extremely ill. My wife was one of the lucky two who did not get sick, which was very helpful to me. My symptoms came on suddenly in the middle of the night and just kept getting worse and worse until I got medical attention. In all, twelve of us suffered waves of nausea and vomiting, and we had abdominal spasms and diarrhea. Most missed two full days of the tour because we were too sick to get out of bed except to dash to the bathroom. It was truly awful. All I wanted to do was just sleep constantly to make the feeling go away. Thanks to my wife's loving care, I found temporary relief from the occasional, tiniest sip of 7-Up. That was all that passed my lips in the right direction!*

Our kind tour leader and driver took us to a Western medical facility in Nairobi. That was where I was tested and confirmed to have amebic dysentery. The medical staff rehydrated me and gave me a shot and a series of pills to treat the condition and make my symptoms bearable. One pair of travelers gave up and returned home at this point, but I resolved to continue. The drive back to our lodging facility was treacherous that night. The roads were pockmarked like the moon, with steep grade changes and poor lighting. Somehow we made it to lodging by midnight. I can still recall lying in the backseat, thankful there was nothing left in my stomach.

By the next evening I was able to eat, but only small amounts of bland food at a time and very slowly and carefully. Twice within six months of returning home I had mysterious flare-ups that put me into the emergency room for rehydration, with apparent food poisoning but no known cause. Never had I been in the emergency room before for intestinal problems, and fortunately never again since those flare-ups. Several years later we met up with one of the other travelers from our safari group. She told us that she had not experienced any long-term problems.

I have not had any stomach problems since. It is funny—before all of this happened I used to say I had a cast-iron stomach!

—Rich Chamberlin, Naperville, IL

1

AMEBIC DYSENTERY, THE BIG PICTURE

The word "dysentery" is used to describe two different stomach illnesses, both of which result in an inflammation of the intestines along with very severe and bloody diarrhea. One form of dysentery is called bacillary dysentery. The other, which is the subject of this book, is called amebic dysentery, also sometimes spelled amoebic dysentery, and also sometimes called amebiasis or intestinal amebiasis. Both forms of dysentery have roughly the same symptoms, and both have a similar cause. They are caused by a parasitic one-celled microorganism, or protozoan. Parasites are organisms that need to feed off of another organism to survive. Microorganisms are organisms such as bacteria that are microscopically small. The difference between

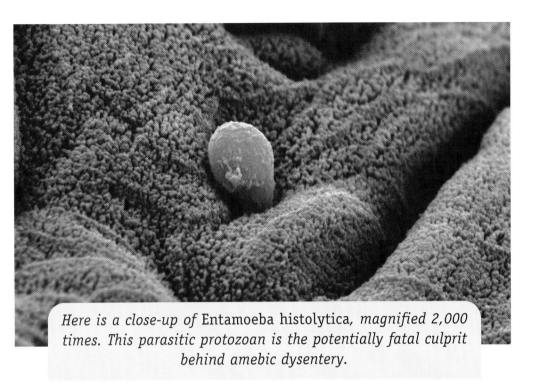

Here is a close-up of Entamoeba histolytica, *magnified 2,000 times. This parasitic protozoan is the potentially fatal culprit behind amebic dysentery.*

the two types of dysentery then comes down to the actual microorganism that causes each type. While bacteria of the genus *Shigella* cause bacillary dysentery, amebic dysentery is caused by a parasite called *Entamoeba histolytica*. Extremely tiny, this shapeless parasite can range in size from ten to sixty micrometers in diameter. This is an extremely small measurement. A micrometer is one millionth of a meter. A meter is 39.37 inches. These parasites are so small you would not be able to see them without the help of a microscope. They move about the large intestine using their pseudopodia, or "false feet," which are simply fingerlike projections. They make their home right there within the walls of the large intestine, and they stay alive by eating red blood cells and small bits of intestinal tissue.

Who Gets Amebic Dysentery?

No one is completely safe from getting sick with amebic dysentery. Whether male or female, young or old, or from any ethnic background, anyone can get amebic dysentery. However, where you live, as well as how healthy you are, have a great deal of influence over whether or not you will get sick from amebic dysentery.

In humans, amebic dysentery is one of the most common diseases caused by a parasite. According to Medline Plus, a service of the National Institutes of Health, about 50 million people get amebic dysentery every year around the world. Between 40,000 and 50,000 people die of amebic dysentery every year.

Not to worry, however! Amebic dysentery is not really a disease that is seen often in the United States and Canada. About 1 to 5 percent of the general population in the United States will get amebic dysentery in any given year. For example, there are about 1,000 cases of amebic dysentery reported in the state of New York every year. The majority of

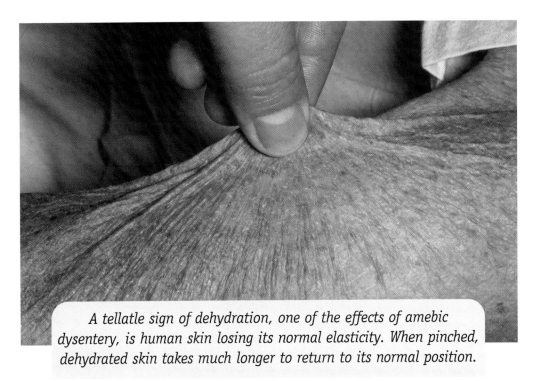

A tellatle sign of dehydration, one of the effects of amebic dysentery, is human skin losing its normal elasticity. When pinched, dehydrated skin takes much longer to return to its normal position.

those cases are in New York City itself. When you consider that the population of New York State is nearly 19 million people, you can see that 1,000 cases of amebic dysentery is really a very small number. In contrast, in some parts of Africa, hundreds of thousands of people will die in any given year due to amebic dysentery and the severe dehydration that often comes with it.

Most Americans and Canadians who get sick with amebic dysentery do so because they had the opportunity to travel overseas and explore far-off lands. The parasite that causes amebic dysentery is most often found in warm, tropical or subtropical climates, especially the warm climates of developing countries. The regions in which one is most likely to find people suffering from amebic dysentery are Mexico and South America, as well as Southeast Asia, India, the Middle East, and the western and southern regions of Africa.

These developing countries have a higher incidence of amebic dysentery because too often the water available for drinking is not kept clean enough and is contaminated with bodily wastes.

Another reason why amebic dysentery is so common in these countries is that farmers tend to use human feces rather than animal feces for the fertilization of their crops. In most countries, farmers use feces from animals, such as cows, as manure. In underdeveloped countries, however, where the population of animals is small and a farmer may only have a handful of animals on his farm, an adequate amount of human feces is more easy to come by than enough animal manure to fertilize an entire crop.

Even if a person is not malnourished, he or she could still get sick with amebic dysentery. This is most likely to happen if the person has some other significant health problems. Research has shown that women who are in their third trimester, or the last three months of pregnancy, have a higher risk of getting amebic dysentery. Elderly people, especially

It is believed that in some areas where amebic dysentery is common, more than half of all the people who live in such areas are most likely carrying the parasite that causes the disease.

those who live in nursing homes, are at higher risk as well. In fact, anyone living in an institutional setting, such as a home for the disabled, has a greater chance of getting amebic dysentery. People who have cancer are also at higher risk of getting sick with amebic dysentery, especially if they are taking cytotoxic medications. These are medicines that are toxic, or poisonous, to certain cells in the body. They prevent the cells from growing or reproducing. People who have cancer take these drugs in an effort to kill off cancer cells or at the very least stop the cancer cells from reproducing.

People who take other prescription drugs called steroids are also more likely to get amebic dysentery, because using steroids lowers a person's resistance to infection. People who may be living in unclean or cramped spaces also have a higher rate of amebic dysentery. People who suffer from alcoholism and people who have suppressed immune systems are also at an increased risk of getting amebic dysentery.

Amebic Dysentery Cysts

Entamoeba histolytica, the parasite that causes amebic dysentery, is transmitted several ways. A person can get amebic dysentery from drinking water that has been contaminated by the parasite while it is still in what is called the cyst stage. A person drinking contaminated water would have no idea that amebic dysentery cysts were in the water, because they are so small.

To become a cyst, an amoeba will roll itself into a sphere shape and secrete a substance that is hard and strong. Wrapping itself in this shell, the amoeba can protect itself. The cyst's tough outer wall or shell keeps it safe from harm against the environment and things that might try to kill it. When in the cyst stage, the parasite is actually not active. The amoeba is considered dormant, or "asleep." Safe within the cyst, it is in this form that the amoeba is transmitted.

Once a cyst makes its way into a person's body, where it is warm and cozy and there is plenty of nourishment, the parasite moves from its inactive cyst stage to an active stage. It "wakes up," so to speak, and can make a person sick.

The cysts, as well as the active amoebas, are found in an infected person's stools. While it can take only one cyst to infect a person, once that cyst is in the body, it multiplies and soon there are many cysts at

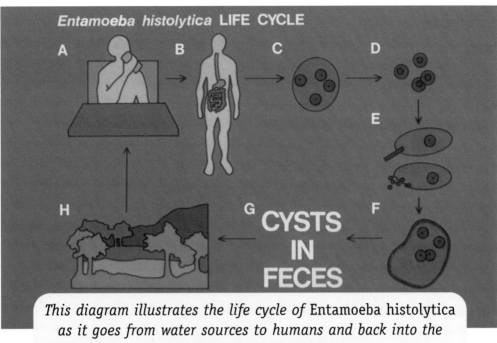

A   B   C   D

E

H   G CYSTS IN FECES   F

This diagram illustrates the life cycle of Entamoeba histolytica *as it goes from water sources to humans and back into the environment once more.*

work making the person sick. The idea behind getting well is to get rid of all the cysts in a person's body. Even though some of the cysts exit the body in the infected person's stools, enough are left behind to continue to cause the person trouble. It will take medicine to completely knock out the cysts from the body for good. At the cyst stage, the parasite is strong enough to live outside the body, whereas at any other stage the parasite would not survive out-side a person's body. So it is the cysts that cause the illness to be transmitted from person to person.

Interestingly, a person who is already getting better or who is only carrying the parasite, but who is not actually suffering from any symptoms, is more likely to spread the illness than a person with an active case of amebic dysentery. Once a person has the misfortune of eating or drinking something contaminated with the cysts, he or she has a good chance of becoming ill because the cysts transform into active amoebas once they reach a human's intestines. Still, the amoebas will not cause much harm if all they do is sit there inside the intestines. The real trouble begins if they get into the walls of the intestines. There they let out enzymes that will dissolve the intestinal mucosa tissue. Once they accomplish this task they can start to eat the red blood cells and tissue and anything else around. They eat by using their pseudopodia to surround and take in their food. When that happens, amebic dysentery is guaranteed. Ulcers in the intestinal mucosa are just the beginning of the damage that can be done.

How Amebic Dysentery Spreads

People who visit or who live in developing countries often come in contact with the parasite by drinking contaminated water, or by cooking or washing with it. Of course, people have no way of knowing whether or not the food or drink they are about to enjoy is infected with a parasite. The microorganisms can get

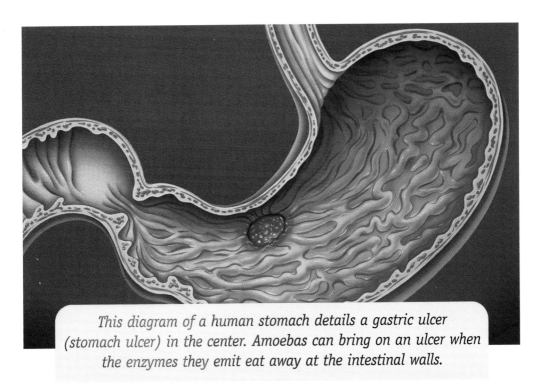

This diagram of a human stomach details a gastric ulcer (stomach ulcer) in the center. Amoebas can bring on an ulcer when the enzymes they emit eat away at the intestinal walls.

into foods and beverages and a person will unknowingly eat or drink them.

Simply washing your hands in contaminated water and then putting your hands in your mouth or touching food with your hands before you eat it can cause you to become infected as well. Even if the water source is clean and clear of the parasite that causes amebic dysentery, foods can still be contaminated by the people preparing them. If those people who prepare food either have the illness themselves or have not washed their hands properly after coming in contact with the microorganism, they can pass the disease along to others through the food they prepare.

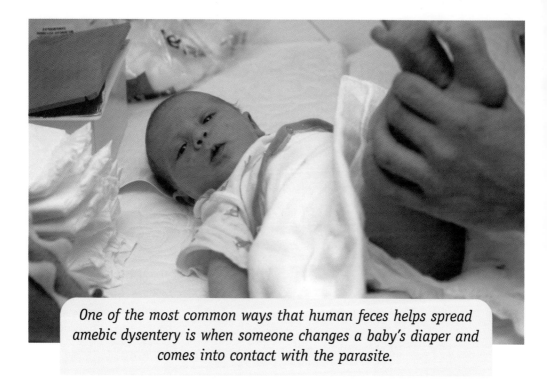

One of the most common ways that human feces helps spread amebic dysentery is when someone changes a baby's diaper and comes into contact with the parasite.

Another way that people can get amebic dysentery is by coming into direct contact with stools from a person who is already infected with amebic dysentery. This is most likely to happen when a person is changing a diaper or cleaning up after a sick person, or in the case of human feces being used as fertilizer in farming.

Flies have occasionally been held responsible for spreading amebic dysentery to food and water in areas where the disease is common. This happens when flies land on and feed off of stools infected with amebic dysentery. There they pick up the cysts of amebic dysentery. They then land on food that will not be washed properly before humans eat it, or they dip their feet in water, contaminating it for the people who will drink it. It is not surprising to learn that cockroaches have also been found guilty of carrying the cysts that cause amebic dysentery.

It is believed that a person needs only to swallow one amebic dysentery–causing cyst to become sick with the disease.

But How?

Once the cysts arrive in the small intestine, they "decyst." Dividing into four amoebas and then again into eight amoebas, the cysts in their new form continue on until they reach the large intestine. Once they reach their destination, like a small enemy army, they strike! This is when the person inside of whom all of this is happening begins to feel the symptoms of amebic dysentery in full force.

Most of the amoebas will leave the body along with the great waves of diarrhea they are causing. Those cysts you just read about are back in civilization and ready to infect others! Through a process of multiplication called binary fission, more cysts are produced. These cysts exit the sick person's body in the stools and are once again out in the open and ready to infect more people. If good hygiene practices are not followed, the cysts will find their way—through water, food, or direct contact—to another person and the cycle will begin again.

Amebic Dysentery as a Sexually Transmitted Disease

It is also believed that certain ways of having sex can cause the spread of amebic dysentery. Sex in which contact with the anus occurs is sometimes thought to be responsible for spreading amebic dysentery. Such sexual activities that may cause amebic dysentery are those in which one partner's mouth comes in direct contact with the anus of a person infected with amebic dysentery. Those activities in which a person puts his or her hands in his or her mouth after touching the anus of a person infected with amebic dysentery can put people at greater risk for developing amebic dysentery as well. Also, activities in which a person puts his or her hands in his or her mouth after touching another object that has touched the anus of a person who has amebic dysentery also puts that person at greater risk.

It is very important to understand that even after a person is no longer sick with the symptoms of amebic dysentery, he or she can still carry the parasite and give it to other people. This is true because the parasite *Entamoeba histolytica* can live in a person's intestines for quite a while even after a person no longer feels sick.

What Does Amebic Dysentery Do?

A very large number—approximately 90 percent—of people who are exposed to the parasite that causes amebic dysentery do not get sick at all. Many others who come in contact with the parasite get sick, but their symptoms are more of an annoyance than a life-threatening situation. It is safe to say that most people who get amebic dysentery do not become dangerously ill. It is interesting to note, however, that those unfortunate enough to get amebic dysentery would generally think of symptoms considered "not especially serious" by medical professionals as "very serious."

After a person comes into contact with the amebic dysentery parasite, he or she may begin suffering from what is considered a mild version of amebic dysentery within as little as a few days to as long as a few months. Most symptoms appear within two to four weeks. He or she may experience nausea, loose stools or diarrhea, weight loss, abdominal tenderness, and fever.

The first and most significant symptom that a person with amebic dysentery will notice is that he or she has a bad case of diarrhea. While diarrhea can be the result of many different illnesses, such as the flu, food poisoning, or even in some cases stress, the diarrhea that people experience when they have amebic dysentery is different.

Amebic dysentery causes diarrhea that has blood, bits of mucus, and even small bits of intestinal tissue in it. The blood comes from ulcers in the intestine. Ulcers are open sores left when tissue has been eaten away. In the case of amebic dysentery, the tissue of the intestines has been eaten away by the amoeba that causes amebic dysentery. The mucus is also a result of these ulcers, which give off pus as well as blood.

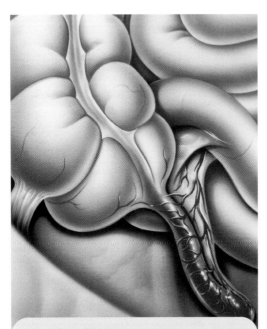

This illustration of a human appendix shows the inflammation that comes from appendicitis.

In addition to this severe diarrhea, a person who has amebic dysentery is likely to have pain and cramps in the abdomen, pain in the rectum, a fever as high as 104 to 105°F (40 to 40.6°C), chills, and a headache. He or she will probably not feel very hungry while sick. This loss of appetite can cause the person to lose weight and even become dehydrated, especially if he or she does not drink enough liquid to replace the large amount of water lost with each episode of diarrhea. Because of all of these symptoms and the fact that diarrhea drains so much from the body, a person who is sick with amebic dysentery is also likely to feel very tired. Sometimes, acute amebic dysentery can also cause complications. A sudden and severe inflammation of the colon, appendicitis (inflammation of the appendix), and a rip or tear, called a perforation, in the wall of the intestines are some of the complications that can be caused by amebic dysentery.

A bout of amebic dysentery usually lasts about two weeks at the most if it is caught right away and treated by a doctor or other medical professional. If caught early, amebic dysentery can be cured and is not likely to come back. If a person cannot get proper medical attention, complications of amebic dysentery can set in. The person is then said to have a chronic case of amebic dysentery. This means that he or she will have symptoms of amebic dysentery over a long period of time or that often these symptoms may seem to go away, but then return. In other words, he or she may have occasional attacks of amebic dysentery. In between these attacks, he or she may have more frequent stomachaches than a

1848
Approximately 11,000 American soldiers serving in the Mexican War die of diseases such as amebic dysentery.

1933
Visitors to the Chicago World's Fair become violently ill, and an outbreak of amebic dysentery is blamed on poor plumbing in a large hotel.

1983
Thirty-eight people are diagnosed with amebic dysentery in Los Angeles County in a four-month period. No source is ever found.

1854–1856
Death from complications of dysentery among Turkish, British, and French soldiers during the Crimean War is ten times more likely than death at the hands of Russian enemies.

1968
A four-year amebic dysentery epidemic begins in Central America killing 20,000.

1983–1992
The United States Centers for Disease Control and Prevention (CDC) reports very few cases in which a person has died from complications of amebic dysentery.

1989 to 1997
Iraq sees an increase in amebic dysentery from 20,000 to 550,000 people.

1993
The CDC reports nearly 3,000 cases of amebic dysentery identified throughout the United States.

1995–1999
Two hundred and thirteen people recently returned from travels abroad are diagnosed with amebic dysentery in Manitoba, Canada.

1991
In Africa, a ten-year period begins during which epidemics of amebic dysentery break out in Tanzania, Zaire, Zambia, Rwanda, Angola, Malawi, Burundi, and Mozambique.

1994–1995
Amebic dysentery declines slowly but steadily since 1984. The CDC votes not to include amebic dysentery in yearly reports.

healthy person would have and may suffer from periods of constipation. The person may also have an enlarged liver and mild to severe damage in the large intestine. Each time an attack occurs, the person will once again suffer from diarrhea, stomach pain, and the rest of the symptoms associated with the disease. Once again the cysts are in the stool and the possibility of infecting others returns. Chronic amebic dysentery can lead to other problems, as well.

If Not Treated Properly . . .

Although severe cases of amebic dysentery are certainly not as common as so-called "mild" cases of the illness, they can happen if the disease is not cared for properly. If left untreated, the amebic dysentery parasite can travel through the body and cause damage to the liver. Once in the liver, amebic dysentery can cause a person to get sick with another serious illness called hepatitis. Hepatitis is a disease caused by a virus in which the liver becomes inflamed and damaged. People who get hepatitis usually have a fever and look a bit yellow in the skin and in the eyes. This yellowing is called jaundice. About 1 percent of all people who get amebic dysentery also develop an abscess on the liver. An abscess is a walled-off area of infection. If these illnesses are not treated properly, the amoebas can continue to spread throughout the body to other vital organs, such as the brain, the lungs, the skin, the diaphragm, the spleen, and the sac that holds the heart, called the pericardium. If the amoebas reach these organs the chance of survival for the sick person decreases greatly.

Every person infected with amebic dysentery will not get this sick. In fact, many people who become infected with amebic dysentery have no symptoms at all. People have been known to carry the parasite for years, often without even knowing it because they never get sick. Although these carriers may feel some mild symptoms, such as occasional stomachaches, they would not have any reason to think their discomfort was due to anything other than something like the flu or eating too much food.

2

AMEBIC DYSENTERY IN HISTORY

It is quite likely that people have been suffering from amebic dysentery since ancient times. Some evidence exists suggesting that amebic dysentery has been around at least since biblical times. The Bible tells of plagues and outbreaks that led to large numbers of people dying. Although the words "amebic dysentery" are never actually seen in the Bible, there is no reason not to think that amebic dysentery was one of the illnesses that caused many people a great deal of suffering and death.

Pasteur, Koch, and the Microbes

Early doctors and scientists had little or no understanding about why and how people got sick. It was not unusual for doctors to reuse their tools and instruments on patient after patient, never washing them between uses. They simply did not understand germs and the way they are transmitted. Today it is widely known that simple hand washing plays an enormous role in keeping people healthy. Before the 1800s, however, very little was known about these things. Many people got sick with infectious diseases such as amebic dysentery and no one knew why it was happening or how to stop it.

By the late 1800s, however, things were changing. Two scientists, a Frenchman named Louis Pasteur and a German man named Robert Koch were working to find out why animals and people got sick. Pasteur discovered microbes and Koch proved how microbes could make a person sick. Dysentery was among the many diseases for which they were able to find causes.

Epidemic!

Even with some evidence of amebic dysentery dating back to Egypt around 500 BC, it is very hard to know exactly when, where, and why the first case of amebic dysentery occurred. Throughout history, this disease has been just one of the difficulties mankind has had to put up with. In years past, an outbreak of amebic dysentery could cause an epidemic. An epidemic is an

Throughout history amebic dysentery has popped up and shown its ugly head on many occasions. Perhaps one of the most common times in which amebic dysentery has been experienced was during the many wars throughout history. Almost every war story has at least one mention of amebic dysentery.

In 1848 during the Mexican War, approximately 11,000 American soldiers who were serving died of various diseases, one of which was amebic dysentery. Only a relatively small number of soldiers, 1,721 of the 90,000 Americans serving in this war, actually died in battle. During the Crimean War between 1854 and 1856, death from complications of dysentery among British, French, and Turkish soldiers was ten times more likely than death by the hands of Russian enemies.

Soldiers often fell sick to stomach trouble thanks to cramped quarters, poor hygiene, dirty water, and lack of proper measures taken to safeguard them against such diseases. Many times a few soldiers would come down with amebic dysentery and before their symptoms would have a chance to express themselves, these soldiers would unknowingly spread the infection to their fellow soldiers. Before it could be stopped, even more soldiers would get sick. With so many soldiers living in such poor conditions, it was often nearly impossible to stop an outbreak of amebic dysentery.

outbreak of a disease that is usually passed from person to person, causing many people to become infected and many people to die. Without proper medicines to stop the illness and without good

A shot of the Columbian Exposition at the 1933 World's Fair in Chicago, Illinois. Polluted drinking water at a hotel serving the event caused the deaths of ninety-eight people.

hygiene to curb the transmission of amebic dysentery, many people died from complications of the infection. The most notable complication to cause death was dehydration.

In 1933, Chicago hosted the World's Fair. Visitors from all over the country, in fact from all over the world, came to see the Chicago World's Fair: A Century of Progress. Poor plumbing in one of the city's large, popular hotels polluted the drinking water that was being supplied to all hotel guests. Many people became violently ill and an outbreak of amebic dysentery was reported. By the end of the outbreak, between 1,400 and 1,700 people from forty-three states, plus Hawaii and Canada, were reported to have come down with amebic dysentery. Of those, ninety-eight people died of the disease. This outbreak was the first waterborne epidemic of amebic dysentery in a civilian population recognized in history. In 1934, as a result of the amebic dysentery outbreak in the city the year before, work was done on the plumbing systems of hotels and mercantile buildings in Chicago. The city hoped the improvements would eliminate further outbreaks of amebic dysentery in Chicago, and they did. Since the 1933 outbreak in Chicago, there has been no major outbreak in the United States. Although occasional cases of amebic dysentery have occurred, these are usually linked to people who handle and prepare food for the public.

In Alaska between 1942 and 1943, a new highway opened. The new Alcan Highway created a pathway for diseases to travel to what was until then a remote, hard-to-reach Native American community. Among the many diseases that came through and spread to remote areas of Alaska was dysentery. Luckily, very few people who became sick actually died.

Today, modern medicine has allowed for excellent treatments for amebic dysentery, which are available especially in the industrialized world. At one time, however, strange things were thought to cure amebic dysentery. Perhaps the strangest report came from

A group from the U.S. Army Corps of Engineers builds the Alcan Highway, which passes through Alaska. Contact with outsiders eventually exposed the indigenous Alaskan people to dysentery.

Brazil. In 1948, it was reported that Brazilians believed garlic was a cure for amebic dysentery!

Are Things Getting Better?

In the United States and Canada, incidents of amebic dysentery have been on a relatively steady decline over the past fifty years or so. Between 1955 and 1964, incidents of amebic dysentery, as reported by the Centers for Disease Control and Prevention (CDC), were still fluctuating. There was a notable rise from 3,689 cases of amebic dysentery reported in the United States in 1956 to 5,031 cases reported in 1957. However, a year later, in 1958, there was a decline to 4,380 cases. The decline continued, steadily dropping back down to roughly the same number in 1964 (3,304 cases) as had been seen in 1955 (3,348 cases). While things were looking good in North America, things were not going as well in Central America. An amebic dysentery epidemic began in Central America in 1968. At the conclusion of its four-year run, 20,000 of the 50,000 people infected had died.

Modern medicine and adequate hygiene had amebic dysentery under control in the United States and Canada for nearly twenty years. But then something strange happened in California in 1983. The Los Angeles County Department of Health Services received word from a nearby medical laboratory that there was a significant increase in the laboratory's diagnoses of amebic dysentery. Between the months of August and October, thirty-eight people had been diagnosed. This rise was significant because the staff at the medical laboratory reported that only about one person per month had been diagnosed with amebic dysentery before August 1983. Even stranger than the mini-outbreak itself was the fact that investigators were unable to trace the common source for the infections. The incident in Los Angeles had been some sort of rare fluke, because following this little incident amebic dysentery was back on the decline in the United States. For the next nine years, between 1983 and 1992, the CDC's "Morbidity and Mortality Weekly Report" reported very few cases in which a person died from complications of amebic dysentery. Although twenty-one deaths were reported in 1983, the number of deaths continued to decrease, rapidly at first, and then steadily until there were only six deaths due to amebic dysentery reported in the United States in 1992.

Unfortunately, during this time other countries continued to not fare as well as the United States and Canada. From 1989 to 1997, infectious diseases increased dramatically in Iraq. Among these diseases was amebic dysentery. Cases of amebic dysentery increased from 20,000 to 550,000, according to a report from March 4, 1998, in the *Gazette*, the daily student newspaper of the University of Western Ontario, Canada.

In Africa, things were not much better. In 1991, a ten-year period began during which epidemics of amebic dysentery broke out in the southern countries of Tanzania, Zaire (present-day Congo), Zambia, Rwanda, Angola, Malawi, Burundi, and Mozambique.

Back in the United States, in 1993 the CDC reported that just 3,000 cases of amebic dysentery had been identified throughout the country. In fact, the relatively slow but nearly steady decline in incidences of amebic dysentery throughout the country since 1985 caused the CDC to make an important decision during 1994–1995. It voted to no longer include national surveillance and cases of amebic dysentery in its yearly reports. The disease is just not one that Americans have to deal with much anymore.

Things look good in Canada, as well. According to the Province of Manitoba Communicable Disease Unit, only 213 people were reported to have been diagnosed with amebic dysentery between 1995 and 1999. This meant there were approximately three to four cases of amebic dysentery seen in every 100,000 people. All of these cases appeared to have been in people who had recently returned from travels abroad.

3

TREATING AMEBIC DYSENTERY

When a person gets amebic dysentery, he or she feels pretty sick. Sometimes people think that whatever is making them sick will just pass. This is quite often true. However, if a person is in or has recently traveled to a country where amebic dysentery is common, there is a good chance he or she may have amebic dysentery and it is important that he or she get professional medical help. Therefore, if a sick person has any of the following symptoms, it is time to call the doctor: severe, liquid diarrhea; bloody or mucous diarrhea; a fever that will not go down; unexplained abdominal pain; pain in the rectum or rectal area; or loss of appetite or unexplained weight loss. A person should also call the doctor if he or she is suffering from a dry mouth, is unusually pale, or notices that his or her eyes look sunken in. These three symptoms are signs of dehydration.

How Do I Know If I Have Amebic Dysentery?

Diarrhea can be very painful to deal with. It can be somewhat frightening at times, too, especially when a person sees blood and mucus in his or her diarrhea. Usually such a discovery is enough to drag a person out of the bathroom and to the phone immediately. Bloody, mucous diarrhea is a definite reason to call the doctor right away!

The doctor will want to know several things before being able to make a diagnosis. First, the doctor will want to know exactly what symptoms the person is suffering from. The doctor will ask questions related to the general health of the person before he or she got sick. The doctor will then ask about the environment in which the sick person lives as well as where he or she works. The doctor will want to know if the sick person has had amebic dysentery at any time in the past and may ask about sexual preferences, practices, and partners. And perhaps most important will be a question about whether or not the sick person has recently traveled to any of the foreign countries in which amebic dysentery is commonly found. That final question is probably the most important and will give the doctor the biggest clue in his or her investigation into the sick person's symptoms.

If the doctor thinks that a person may have a case of amebic dysentery after asking all of the important questions, the doctor will ask for a stool sample in order to run tests. This sample can be collected either right away in a bathroom within the office, or a few hours later in the sick person's own home. Collecting a stool sample is a rather unpleasant task. If the sick person is lucky, all he or she will have to do is use a large plastic bowl instead of the toilet when feeling the need to pass a stool. The bowl, tightly covered with a lid, can then be brought back to the doctor's office or a laboratory so the stool can be analyzed. Some people are asked to take a more active role in providing their samples. After using the plastic bowl, they are directed to use a small plastic spoonlike stick to scoop a small amount of stool into one or more small vials containing a specially prepared liquid. Once these samples are prepared, they can be brought back to the doctor or to the lab for testing.

Another way that the doctor may look for amebic dysentery is by swabbing the rectal area of the sick person. Either way, the stool sample will be looked at

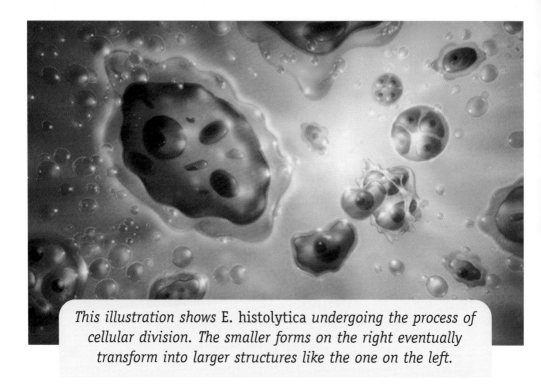

This illustration shows E. histolytica *undergoing the process of cellular division. The smaller forms on the right eventually transform into larger structures like the one on the left.*

carefully under a microscope. The doctor or technician examining the stool sample will be able to see certain forms of the amoebas that cause amebic dysentery, if the person is in fact infected. The doctor or technician may also look for the cysts that cause amebic dysentery as a way of making a definite diagnosis. If the doctor knows that the patient has dysentery, but is not completely certain which type it is, the doctor may have to swab a small sample from the intestines of the sick person. From this sample, the doctor will be able to determine which microorganism is causing the dysentery and therefore which type of dysentery the person has.

Unfortunately, it can sometimes be a bit difficult for medical personnel to diagnose amebic dysentery. The reason for this is that the symptoms of amebic dysentery can be similar to the symptoms of other stomach illnesses. A common illness that amebic dysentery is often confused with is infection of *Entamoeba coli*. The symptoms of the illnesses are similar, so it might be confusing for a medical professional to decide which illness a person has without doing very specific testing.

Taking Care of Sickness

The first thing to know about treating amebic dysentery is that people should not try to treat it themselves. Often, people who have diarrhea will buy an over-the-counter medicine, such as loperamide, the active ingredient in Immodium or Pepto-Bismol, which are meant to control or stop diarrhea. It can be dangerous for a person with amebic dysentery to take these medications because by stopping the diarrhea the person is actually stopping the parasite from leaving his or her body. This can make the person much sicker, even if at first he or she feels better because the diarrhea has temporarily stopped.

There are a few different medicines that doctors can give to a person who has amebic dysentery. Several types of drugs are commonly used together for treating the disease. An antibiotic is used to fight bacterial infection. Another drug called an amebicide, or an antiparasitic, is given to rid the intestines of the parasite. Drugs with names like tetracycline, metronidazole, paromomycin, emetine, and diiodohydroxyquin (also called iodoquinol) are the most common drugs used to treat amebic dysentery.

In addition to these medicines, the doctor will also want to take care of the dehydration that frequently occurs when a person has amebic dysentery. To treat dehydration, the sick person is given fluids to replace the fluids he or she has lost through the diarrhea. If the sick person can drink without throwing up or having more diarrhea, he or she will be given things like water and juice or preparations similar to a

Pink bismuth is the generic term for the medical remedy that contains loperamide. It is also sold under several brand names.

sports drink that are filled with a balance of electrolytes and salts. However, if taking only a few sips causes the person to have more diarrhea, he or she will need intravenous fluids. To give intravenous, or IV, fluids, a small needle will be inserted into one of the patient's veins, usually a vein in the arm or the back of the hand. The needle sets a small plastic tube in place and is then removed. Attached to the small tube is a long piece of flexible plastic tubing. At the other end of that tubing will be a clear bag of liquid, which hangs from a pole. The liquid in the bag is made up of water, salts, and electrolytes. The right balance of these is

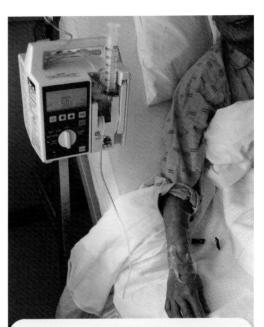

Severe cases of amebic dysentery often require that the patient is fed intravenously.

important, as it must closely match the balance the person's body would normally make if he or she were not sick. Once the person is rehydrated, he or she will begin to feel better.

In the case of a great deal of blood loss, a person may need to have a blood transfusion to replace the blood lost.

Doctor, Will I Live?

For the most part, people who get amebic dysentery do well with rehydration, rest, reintroduction of healthful foods, and the medicines prescribed by their doctors. However, the real prognosis for a person who has amebic dysentery is based on several things. Possibly the most important factor in deciding whether the person will recover or not is based on where he or she lives. A traveler who catches amebic dysentery while on an adventurous vacation will probably be able to enjoy the rest of his or her trip, as the symptoms are not likely to come on until after he or she returns home (depending on the length of the trip and the point of infection, of course). The traveler will likely do well if treated either in a Westernized hospital in the foreign country of his or her travels, or in a hospital back home if the amebic dysentery develops after the vacation is over. A person who lives in an underdeveloped country where amebic dysentery is common may not have a good hospital or appropriate medicines available. Such a person is not as likely to make a full recovery. Other factors, such as how healthy the person was before he or she got sick with amebic dysentery and where the infection has located itself within the person's body also make a difference on how well the person responds to treatment. For the most part, prognosis for anyone who gets amebic dysentery is initially considered good. However, if the disease has a chance to spread to other organs and cause serious problems such as those mentioned before, like infection in the liver or a perforated intestinal wall (also called a perforated bowel), there is an increased chance that

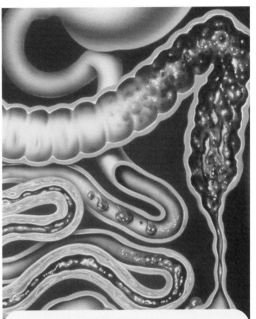

Another result of extended bouts of amebic dysentery is fulminating colitis, which affects the colon, pictured here.

the person could die. About half of all people whose amebic dysentery advances to a severe inflammation of the colon, a condition called fulminating colitis, are likely to die.

Amebic dysentery strikes each person differently and many factors will be considered in evaluating a person's chances for survival. In fact, the range of these factors can be as broad and varied as the long list of complications caused by the disease itself.

FIGHTING THE FURY

Basic hygiene is the key to preventing amebic dysentery. Good, frequent hand washing with soap and warm water, especially after using the bathroom and before eating or preparing food for others, is extremely important in preventing the transmission of many diseases, not only amebic dysentery. However, no matter how careful a person is with washing his or her hands and following all precautions against amebic dysentery, no measure will be enough unless the water supply is clean.

If you plan to travel to places that are known to have high rates of amebic dysentery there are a number of things you can do that will greatly reduce your risk of becoming ill.

When traveling in countries or regions known to have high rates of amebic dysentery, it is imperative to avoid eating food from street vendors.

⊛ Only drink bottled water or water that has been boiled and then cooled to drinking temperature.

⊛ Never use ice cubes unless they are made with bottled water or boiled water.

⊛ Continue to use the bottled water or boiled water to brush your teeth, wash your hands, wash food, and cook food.

⊛ No matter how tempting it may be to taste local foods, never eat food from street vendors. There is no way of knowing whether or not the vendors have used contaminated water when they cooked their food.

- Avoid drinking milk and eating cheese because they may not have been pasteurized.

- Be sure that all the food you eat has been cooked to a high temperature and it has not been left to cool to room temperature since it was cooked.

- Never eat raw fruit or vegetables, unless you can peel them for yourself.

Boiling water that is infected with amebic dysentery can kill the cysts if tablets of tetraglycine hydroperiodide are added. One or two tablets added to each quart (liter) of boiling water are usually enough to kill any cysts that may be going for a swim. Chlorine, however, which is commonly used to keep swimming pools clean and as a cleaner against bacteria, will not kill the cysts that cause amebic dysentery.

Keeping the Whole Family Safe

Unfortunately, once one person gets amebic dysentery, it is quite possible that everyone in a family will get it, too. This is especially a problem when there is a large number of people living in a very small amount of space with poor opportunities for keeping clean. However, under normal circumstances, it is not too

There are two main ways for a person to lower his or her risk of getting sick with amebic dysentery when having sex with a person who is infected. The first way is by using a latex condom for anal contact. The second way is by keeping the mouth and hands away from the anus of the sexual partner. It is important to follow both of these rules when engaging in sexual activity with a person who has, or might have, amebic dysentery.

hard to keep the rest of the family safe and prevent a family outbreak of amebic dysentery. The two most important things for the infected person to do if he or she wants to keep the rest of the family healthy are simple. The person must see a doctor and follow his or her instructions, taking all the medicines prescribed. And he or she must always remember to wash his or her hands often, but especially before handling or preparing food, after a trip to the bathroom, and after changing a diaper. Warm water and soap are the infected person's best friends at this point!

Amebic Dysentery and the Future

With all of the medications available to treat amebic dysentery, most people who get this illness are in pretty good shape. That is, of course, if they live in a country where such medicines are available. In developing countries where medicine is not as easy to come by as it is in the developed parts of the world, such as the United States, Canada, and Europe, some people still become very ill when they get amebic dysentery. Aside from improving the overall conditions of water and sanitation throughout the world, another way to keep everyone safe from amebic dysentery would be for scientists to find a cure for the disease. What might be even better would be a vaccine against the illness.

Currently, there is neither a cure for nor a vaccine against amebic dysentery. A vaccine might be more helpful than a cure because if everyone were vaccinated against amebic dysentery, in the manner in which nearly everyone is now vaccinated against polio, no one would get amebic dysentery anymore, just as people no longer get polio. The vaccine would then, in effect, become a cure. Scientists are currently working on a few different possible vaccines and will hopefully have one available before long.

For now, however, while there are no cures or vaccines, people must rely only on prevention and treatment of amebic dysentery. Education about amebic dysentery, how it is spread, and how it can be prevented is also key. It is important for people traveling to underdeveloped countries to understand what precautions they need to take to avoid getting sick with amebic dysentery. It is also important for travelers to know the symptoms of the illness and to understand the importance of getting medical attention right away. And it is important for those who are at risk for amebic dysentery due to sexual practices or because of where they live or work to understand how and why amebic dysentery is spread so that they can keep themselves as safe as possible. Making sure people understand the risks so that they can take good care of themselves is often the job of doctors, nurses, or other health officials. Understanding who is at risk for getting amebic dysentery, what the symptoms are, and how to treat it are the tools for creating a cleaner, healthier world.

GLOSSARY

acidic Sour.

acute Severe; developing quickly and lasting a
   short time.

antibiotic A substance produced by microorganisms, and especially by bacteria and fungi,
   that is used to kill or prevent the growth of
   harmful germs.

anus The opening at the lower end of the large
   intestines through which solid waste exits
   the body.

bacteria Any of numerous microscopic plants that
   are single celled and whose chemical activities
   can either be harmful or beneficial to humans.

binary fission Reproduction by division into
   two parts.

chronic Continuing for a long time or returning often.

colon The main part of the large intestine.

cytotoxic medications Medicines that are toxic, or poisonous, to cells and prevent them from growing or reproducing.

diaphragm A muscular wall that separates the chest from the abdomen.

electrolyte A substance, such as an acid or a salt, that when dissolved, such as in water, conducts an electric current.

intravenous In the vein.

jaundice A yellowing of the skin and eyes caused by liver illness.

microorganism An organism, such as a bacterium, that is microscopically small.

parasite A typically harmful plant or animal that lives in or on another living thing and gets food and sometimes shelter from it.

pasteurized When a liquid has been kept for a time at a temperature high enough to kill many harmful germs and then cooled rapidly.

perforation A rip or tear.

polio A once common viral disease that affected children, often causing paralysis.

prognosis A forecast concerning the probable course of an illness and the chances of recovery.

protozoan Any of a large group of mostly microscopic animals whose bodies are single cells.

rectum The last section of the large intestine.

vaccine A material containing killed or weakened bacteria or viruses used in protecting against disease.

FOR MORE INFORMATION

Centers for Disease Control and Prevention
1600 Clifton Road
Atlanta, GA 30333
(800) 311-3435
Web site: http://www.cdc.gov

National Institutes of Health
9000 Rockville Pike
Bethesda, MD 20892
Web site: http://www.nih.gov

World Health Organization
Regional Office for the Americas/Pan American
    Health Organization (AMRO/PAHO)
525 23rd Street NW
Washington, DC 20037
(202) 974-3000
Web site: http://www.who.int

In Canada

Health Canada
A.L. 0900C2
Ottawa, ON K1A 0K9
(613) 957-2991
Web site: http://www.hc-sc.gc.ca

Web Sites

Due to the changing nature of Internet links, the Rosen Publishing Group, Inc., has developed an online list of Web sites related to the subject of this book. This site is updated regularly. Please use this link to access the list:

http://www.rosenlinks.com/epid/amdy

FOR FURTHER READING

Cartwright, Frederick F., and Michael Biddiss. *Disease and History*. London: Sutton Publishing, 2000.

Giblin, James Cross. *When Plague Strikes: The Black Death, Smallpox, AIDS*. New York: Harper-Collins, 1995.

Klein, Aaron E. *The Parasites We Humans Harbor*. New York: Elsevier/Nelson Books, 1981.

Mulcahy, Robert. *Diseases: Finding the Cure*. Minneapolis: Oliver Press, Inc., 1996.

Nourse, Alan E. *Viruses*. New York: Franklin Watts, 1976.

Nourse, Alan E. *The Virus Invaders*. New York: Franklin Watts, 1992.

Nourse, Alan E. *Your Immune System*. New York: Franklin Watts, 1982.

Perlin, David, and Ann Cohen. *The Complete Idiot's Guide to Dangerous Diseases and Epidemics.* Indianapolis: Alpha, 2002.

Preston, Richard. *The Hot Zone.* New York: Anchor, 1995.

Zim, Herbert S. *Your Stomach and Digestive Tract.* New York: William Morrow & Co., 1973.

INDEX

A

abdominal tenderness/pain,
    21, 22, 26, 27, 37
Africa, 11, 12, 25, 35
Alaska, 32
alcoholism, 13
amebic dysentery
    acute, 23
    cause of, 8, 9, 14
    chronic, 23, 26
    death from, 10, 11, 24, 27,
        30, 31, 32, 34, 35, 45
    diagnosis of, 38–41
    history of, 29–32
    people/places at risk,
        12–13, 20
    preventing, 47–50
    as a sexually transmitted
        disease, 20
    spread/transmission of,
        14–16, 16–19, 20, 31

statistics on, 10, 11, 21,
    33–34, 35–36
symptoms of, 21–26, 27,
    37–38
treatment of, 41–44
amebicide, 42
Angola, epidemic in,
    25, 35
antibiotics, 42
antiparasitic, 42
appendicitis, 23
appetite, loss of, 22–23, 37

B

bacillary dysentery, 8, 9
binary fission, 19
blood
    in diarrhea, 8, 22, 37, 38
    loss of, 44
blood transfusion, 44
Burundi, epidemic in, 25, 35

C

Canada/Canadians, 10, 11, 25, 32, 33, 34, 35, 36, 51

cancer, 13

Centers for Disease Control and Prevention, 24, 25, 33, 35, 36
"Morbidity and Mortality Weekly Report," 35

Central America, epidemic in, 24, 34

Chicago's World's Fair, 24, 31–32

chills, 22

chlorine, 49

cockroaches, spread of disease by, 19

colon, inflammation of, 23, 45

constipation, 26

Crimean War, 24, 30

cysts, 14–16, 18, 19–20, 26, 40, 49

cyst stage, 14, 15

cytotoxic medications, 13

D

decysting, 19

dehydration, 11, 23, 31
symptoms of, 38
treatment of, 42–43

developing/underdeveloped countries, 16, 44

incidence of amebic dysentery in, 12
traveling to, 51–52

diapers, changing, 18, 50

diarrhea, 19, 21–22, 23, 26, 37, 38, 42, 43
blood/mucus in, 8, 22, 37, 38
over-the-counter medications for, 41

diiodohydroxyquin, 42

dysentery, types of, 8–9

E

Egypt, 29

elderly people, 12–13

emetine, 42

Entamoeba coli, 41

Entamoeba histolytica, 9, 14, 21

epidemic, definition of, 29–30

Europe, 51

F

fatigue, 23

fertilizer, human feces as, 12, 18

fever, 21, 22, 26, 37

flies, spread of disease by, 18–19

food preparation, 16–17, 18–19, 32, 47, 48, 50

fulminating colitis, 45

Acknowledgment

I wish to thank Richard Chamberlin for offering to tell his story and then for following through. Thank you so much for your help! I also wish to thank the members of SCBWI for their support and for being such an assisting network. Thanks also to Mindy S. Apel and her keen eye. And, as always, I thank my family for their love and support, despite their ongoing stomachaches!

About the Author

Melanie Ann Apel has written more than forty nonfiction books for children and young adults. She holds a bachelor's degree in theatre arts from Bradley University and another in respiratory care from National-Louis University. Melanie and her family live in Chicago, Illinois.

Photo Credits

Cover and chapter title interior photos © M. Peres/CMSP; p. 4 © AFP/Corbis; p. 9 © Eye of Science/Photo Researchers, Inc.; p. 11 © NMSB/CMSP; p. 15 © Educational Images/CMSP; p. 17 © John Bavosi/Photo Researchers, Inc.; p. 18 © CMSP; pp. 22, 45 © John Bavosi/Science Photo Library/Photo Researchers, Inc.; p. 31 © Bettmann/Corbis; p. 33 © Grant MacDonald/AP/Wide World Photos; p. 40 © Jim Dowdalls/Science Source/Photo Researchers, Inc.; p. 42 © D. A. Weinstein/CMSP; p. 43 © M. Kalab/CMSP; p. 48 © Serge Attal/Timepix.

Designer: Evelyn Horovicz; Editor: Eliza Berkowitz